Common Core
ENGLISH GRAMMAR
& Mechanics

1

Nancy L. McGraw
Nancy Tondy
Regina Webb

Joan Archer
Diane Dillon
Patricia Kecskemety

Bright Ideas Press, LLC
Cleveland, OH

Summer Solutions
Common Core
English Grammar & Mechanics 1

All rights reserved. No part of this publication may be reproduced or transmitted in any form or by any means, electronic or mechanical, including photocopy, recording, or any information storage or retrieval system. Reproduction of these materials for an entire class, school, or district is prohibited.

Printed in the United States of America

The writers of *Summer Solutions* Common Core English Grammar & Mechanics aligned the series in accordance with information from the following:

National Governors Association Center for Best Practices,
Council of Chief State School Officers.
Common Core State Standards, English Language Arts.
National Governors Association Center for Best Practices,
Council of Chief State School Officers, Washington, D.C., 2010.

ISBN: 978-1-60873-058-2

Cover Design: Dan Mazzola
Editor: Christopher Backs

Copyright © 2015 by Bright Ideas Press, LLC
Cleveland, Ohio

Instructions for Parents / Guardians

- *Summer Solutions* is an extension of the *Simple Solutions* Approach being used by thousands of children in schools across the United States.

- This summer book aligns with the English Language Arts Common Core State Standards, which identify key ideas, understandings, and skills appropriate for this particular grade level. The Common Core State Standards addressed in this book are listed on the next page.

- The 30 lessons included in each workbook are meant to review and reinforce the skills learned in the grade level just completed.

- The program is designed to be used three days per week for ten weeks to ensure retention. Completing the book all at one time defeats the purpose of sustained practice over the summer break.

- Check each lesson immediately after completion by using the answer key in the back of the book. Go over any items that were difficult or done incorrectly.

- Adjust the use of the book to fit vacations. More lessons may have to be completed during the weeks before or following a family vacation.

Summer Solutions
Common Core
English Grammar & Mechanics 1

Reviewed Skills Include · Standard

- Use common, proper, and possessive nouns L.1.1b
- Use singular and plural nouns with matching verbs L.1.1c
- Use personal, possessive, and indefinite pronouns L.1.1d
- Use verbs to convey a sense of past, present, and future L.1.1e
- Use frequently occurring adjectives L.1.1f
- Produce and expand complete simple and compound sentences L.1.1j
- Capitalize dates and names of people L.1.2a
- Use end punctuation for sentences L.1.2b
- Use commas in dates and words in a series L.1.2c
- Use conventional spelling for words with common spelling patterns L.1.2d
- Use frequently occurring affixes as a clue to the meaning of a word L.1.4b
- Identify frequently occurring root words L.1.4c
- Recognize the distinguishing features of a sentence RF.1.1a
- Know the spelling-sound correspondences for common consonant digraphs RF.1.3a
- Determine the number of syllables in a printed word RF.1.3d

Answers to Lessons begin on page 63.

Lesson #1

1. Write the days correctly.

   tuesday _____

   saturday _____

   monday _____

2. Give each sentence end punctuation.

   She has a globe __

   Where do you live __

   Did you meet the new teacher __

3. **A *noun* is a naming word. A noun can name a person, a place, or a thing.** Circle the nouns that name things.

   library

   cup

   school

   hat

   girl

   mouse

4. Write the missing letters to spell words with the **short a** sound.

h__m   f__n   h__nd   b__nd

5. Write a sentence about the picture. Use the words in the box.

| is | Mitch | mailing | his |
| a | grandmother | to | letter |

_____

_____.

6. Choose a verb that tells about the past.

Last week, we _____ to the circus.

goes   went   will go

3

Lesson #2

1. A *pronoun* can take the place of any noun. *He, she, it,* and *they* are pronouns.
   Examples: The boy runs. → **He** runs.
   My sister is tall. → **She** is tall.

   Use **he**, **she**, **it**, or **they** to take the place of the words below.

   Bill → _____

   the dishes → _____

2. Choose the correct word.

   We (is / are) tired from the trip.

   You (is / are) nice.

3. **Describing words are called *adjectives*. They tell *how many, what color, the size,* or *the shape* of something.**
   Examples: green short big two old

   Underline an **adjective** in the sentence below.

   We have a tall family.
   (What kind of family?)

4. **A date tells the month, the number of the day, and the year. Always put a <u>comma</u> between the day and the year.**
   Example: April 16, 2008

   Put a comma between the day and the year.

   June 10 2007   March 30 2016

5. Read all of the words. Draw a line to connect the naming part with the action part.

   A flat tire   remember your lunch?

   Tammy and Jessie   does not roll.

   Did you   are sisters.

6. Add a suffix. Write the missing word.

   -ful   -less   -er

   A flat tire is !
   (use)

Lesson #3

1. Add the suffix. Write the new word.

Base Word	-ed	-ing
brush	_____	_____
water	_____	_____
bark	_____	_____

2. Circle pictures of words that begin with **wh**.

3. Study the list of words. Circle the words that should begin with a capital letter.

   december   chris   cookie   friday

   henry   dish   wagon   august

4. Put a check next to the sentence that has correct end punctuation.

___ There are many kinds of clouds!

___ Did you watch that show on storms.

___ I am afraid of storms!

5. Circle the nouns that name people.

mom

park

teacher

man

tiger

eagle

6. Say each word. Write the number of syllables.

family ___   mother ___   house ___

Lesson #4

1. **The "a–consonant–e" pattern spells the long a sound.** Write the missing letters to spell words with the **long a** sound.

    t_p_ r__k__ sn__k__ c__n__

2. Choose a verb to tell what will happen next.

    The chicks are hungry. The mother is looking for food. The chicks _____.

    are eating   will eat   ate

3. Use **he**, **she**, **it**, or **they** to take the place of the words below.

    Grandpa → _____

    the sled → _____

4. Write a sentence about the picture. Use the words in the box.

| good | I | oven | cooking |
| something | smell | the | in |

_____

_____.

5. Choose the correct word.

They (is / are) at the zoo today.

You (is / are) the last one in line.

6. **An adjective can tell *how many*.** Circle the words that tell how many.

three birds   many children   one candy cane

seven dogs   few kittens   five rings

Lesson #5

1. Put a comma between the names in the list.

   Julie_ Tess_ Pam_ and Marta are my sisters.

2. Add a suffix. Write the missing word.

   -ful   -er   -ed

   The dog is _____ with his ball.
   (play)

3. Double the final consonant. Add a suffix. Write the new word.

Base Word	-ed	-ing
rob	_____	_____
trim	_____	_____
drip	_____	_____

4. **A sentence must have an end mark or end punctuation. A sentence must begin with a capital letter.** Circle the sentence that is correct.

My dad is my soccer coach.

can I play?

Ask your mom

5. Fill in the missing letters. Write **th** or **ch**.

clo___ ___   in___ ___

6. Say each word. Write the number of syllables.

basketball ___   net ___   shoes ___

Lesson #6

1. Put a comma between the words in the list.

    Jamie read a book about tigers bears lions and elephants.

2. Write the correct end punctuation mark. Use a period, a question mark, and an exclamation point.

    I can't believe it is so hot __

    Do you think we can go inside __

    I need a cold drink before I get sick __

3. Finish the story. Write a verb in each sentence.

    | will rake   are falling   raked |

    Yesterday, Kelly _____ the yard.

    Today, more leaves _____.

    Tomorrow, Kelly _____ the yard again.

4. Read the sentence below. Circle the name that should begin with a capital letter. Write it correctly on the line.

ricardo was at the playground.

_____

5. Write the missing letters to spell words with the **short e** sound.

j___t   t___nt   b___d   l___mon

6. **A proper noun names a particular person, place, or thing and always begins with a capital letter.** Underline the proper nouns.

sister   Julie   girl

Ohio   playground   Maple Street

Lesson #7

1. Use **he, she, it,** or **they** to take the place of the words below.

    Mrs. Smith → _____

    a monkey → _____

    the bushes → _____

2. Choose the correct word.

    They (is / are) the neighbors.

    She (is / are) in my class at school.

3. **An adjective can tell *what color*.** Circle the words that tell what color.

    (red) balloon   green fence

    yellow ball   purple grape

    pink pen   blue sky

4. Make one sentence that tells about the picture.

   It is snowing. I catch snowflakes on my tongue.

   _____

   _____

5. Put a comma between the day and year.

   June 3 2005   September 10 2017

   May 21 2013   July 5 2011

6. The pictures show words that have the **sh** sound. Connect each word to its picture.

   brush   trash   bush

Lesson #8

1. Add a suffix. Don't forget to double the consonant. Write the missing word.

   -ing   -er   -ed

   The toad _____ into the pond.
   (hop)

2. **Add -ed to a verb to show something happened already.** Fill in the missing words.

   spell   race   want

   Juan _____ home after school.

   He _____ to hurry and tell his mom that

   he _____ the last word correctly and won the spelling bee.

3. Say each word. Write the number of syllables.

   beginning ___   sunrise ___   rooster ___

4. Write the correct end punctuation mark. Use a period, a question mark, and an exclamation point.

The backpack is still in the car___

My favorite show is on tonight___

When will you get to go___

5. There are 3 words that should begin with a capital letter. Circle the letters that should be capital.

dr. torres gave the glasses to nora.

6. Underline the subject of the sentence.

The children caught fireflies.

Lesson #9

1. **The "ee" pattern spells the long e sound.** Write the missing letters to spell words with the **long e** sound.

b__ __   tr__ __   sh__ __p   j__ __p

2. Underline the noun in this sentence.

   The train moves slowly.

3. Make one sentence that tells about the picture.

   Our team is winning. The fans are cheering.

   _____

   _____

4. Choose a verb that tells about now.

   The little dog _____ a hat.

   wore   wears   will wear

5. Use **he**, **she**, **it**, or **they** to take the place of the words below.

   Greg → _____

   a goat → _____

6. The pictures show words with the **wh** sound. Connect each word to its picture.

   whisker   whisper   wheel

Lesson #10

1. Choose the correct word.

    The boy (is / are) in second grade.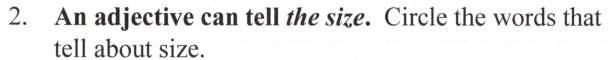

    We (is / are) fishing at the lake.

2. **An adjective can tell *the size*.** Circle the words that tell about size.

    (tiny) ants   big house

    huge truck   small dog

    tall tree   short pencil

3. Put a comma between the colors in the list.

    Karen had pink yellow blue and orange hair clips.

4. Add a suffix. Write the missing word.

   -ful   -ing   -ed

   We say what we're _____
   for on Thanksgiving.   (thank)

5. Write a sentence about the picture.
   Use the words in the box.

   | red   The   away   flew   balloon |

   _____

   _____.

6. Double the final consonant. Add a suffix. Write the new word.

   Base Word   -ed   -ing

   spot   _____   _____

   shop   _____   _____

21

Lesson #11

1. Use the words in the box to make 2-syllable words.

pop	fruit	grape
cake	cup	corn

   _____ _____ _____

2. Fill in.

   question mark   period   exclamation point

   A _____ comes at the end of a statement.

   Questions end with a _____ _____.

   A statement that shows excitement ends with a(n)_____ _____.

3. Circle the words that should begin with a capital letter.

   blue   connor   august   clock   monday

4. Write the missing letters to spell words with the **short i** sound.

p___g   b___b   p___n   d___g

5. **A proper noun names a special thing and always begins with a capital letter.** Which are proper nouns?

book   *Charlotte's Web*   street

Uncle Pete   school   Africa

6. Choose the verb that shows something will happen later.

Soon, the sad cat _____ some milk.

has   had   will have

Lesson #12

1. Use **he, she, it,** or **they** to take the place of the words below.

   Mrs. Jones → _____

   the chickens → _____

2. Make one sentence that tells about the picture.

   We went to the fair. We rode the rides.

   _____

   _____

   _____

3. Choose the correct word.

   Mom (is / are) driving us home.

   We (is / are) happy to see her.

4. Underline an **adjective** in the sentence below.

A cat has sharp claws.

5. Insert the commas where they are needed.

June 6 2017   May 4 2012

February 14 2015   August 1 2014

6. The pictures show words that have the **ch** sound. Write each **ch** word under its picture.

chick   bunch   chips

_____   _____   _____

Lesson #13

1. Add a suffix. Write the missing word.

    -ful   -less   -ing

    A cup with a hole is _____.
    (use)

2. Underline the group of words that makes a sentence.

    A bucket

    We play in the sand.

3. **Add –ed to a verb to show something happened already.** Fill in the missing words.

    place   show   clap

    Eli _____ the team his new bat.

    Everyone _____ when he hit a home run.

    He _____ the bat in the bag after the game.

4. Use the words in the box to make 2-syllable words.

| sea | fish | town |
| star | horse | down |

_____ _____ _____

5. Add the correct end punctuation to each sentence.

Mark had a bonfire last night__

We cooked marshmallows__

I burned mine__

6. **The "i–consonant–e" pattern spells the long i sound.** Write the missing letters to spell words with the **long i** sound.

k__t__   br__d__   v__n__   p__p__

Lesson #14

1. Write the days correctly.

   friday _____

   tuesday _____

2. **A *noun* can name a person.** Underline the noun that names a person.

   My brother threw the ball.

3. Look at the picture, then complete each sentence. Use the words in the box.

   | got   is reading   will read |

   Tomorrow, Mary _____ the book.

   Today, Mary _____ the book.

   Yesterday, Mary _____ the book.

4. Use **he, she, it,** or **they** to take the place of the words below.

Maria → _____

the basket → _____

5. Choose the correct word.

My sisters (was / were) sick.

The house (was / were) old.

6. Make one sentence that tells about the picture.

We built a snowman. We gave it a carrot nose.

_____

_____

_____

Lesson #15

1. Underline an **adjective** in the sentence below.

   Billy gave me a blue pencil.

2. Put a comma between the names in the list.

   Greg Jack Tim and Doug are in my class.

3. Circle pictures of words that begin with the **kn** sound.

4. Add a prefix. Write the missing word.

   re-   un-   pre-

   Tim went to _____
   last year.   (school)

5. Write a sentence about the picture.
   Use the words in the box.

   | wind   the   A   sailboat   blew |

   _____

   _____

6. Double the final consonant. Add a suffix. Write the new word.

   Base Word   -ed   -ing

   nap   _____   _____

   beg   _____   _____

   stop   _____   _____

Lesson #16

1. Use the words in the box to make 2-syllable words.

week	tub	ball
bath	foot	end

   _____ _____ _____

2. Put a check in the box next to the sentences that have incorrect end punctuation. In the next box put the correct punctuation.

   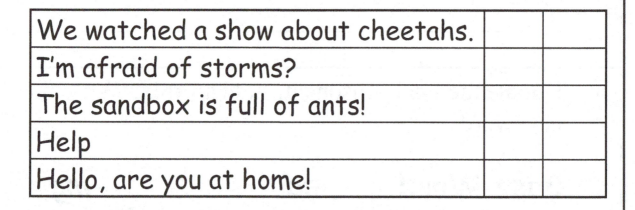

Sentence		
We watched a show about cheetahs.		
I'm afraid of storms?		
The sandbox is full of ants!		
Help		
Hello, are you at home!		

3. Circle the name that should begin with a capital letter. Write it correctly on the line.

   The teacher helped betsy.

   _____

4. Write the missing letters to spell words with the **short o** sound.

f_x   r__ck   b__x   m__p

5. Underline the noun that names a place.

Our class went to the park.

6. Choose the verb that shows something will happen later.

Soon, the ants _____.

will eat   ate   eats

Lesson #17

1. Use **he**, **she**, **it**, or **they** to take the place of the words below.

    the boxes → _____

    her sister → _____

2. Choose the correct word.

    The see-saw (was / were) empty.

    The ducks (was / were) white.

3. Make one sentence that tells about the picture.

    We went to the zoo.
    We saw giraffes and elephants.

    _____

    _____

    _____ .

4. Circle the words that tell the shape of something.

(flat) pancakes   round peaches   long snake

oval track   wavy line   curved road

5. Put a comma between the words in the list.

Kathy has soccer practice on Tuesday Wednesday Thursday and Saturday.

6. Fill in the missing letters. Write **th** or **ch**.

bro__ __   pea__ __   too__ __

Lesson #18

1. Add a prefix. Write the missing word.

   un-   pre-   re-

   I want to _____ the walls.   (paint)

2. Underline the group of words that makes a sentence.

   We ate ice cream.

   in a cone.

   I like vanilla

3. Double the final consonant. Add a suffix. Write the new word.

Base Word	-ed	-ing
rip	_____	_____
roll	_____	_____
drag	_____	_____

4. Give each sentence the correct end punctuation.

Yea, we got our new bikes today___

I think I want chocolate___

Why don't you get one too___

5. Write the months correctly.

january _____

june _____

april _____

6. Say each word. Write the number of syllables.

period ___   capital ___   alphabet ___

Lesson #19

1. Fill in the missing letters to spell words with the **long o** sound.

   s__ __p   h__s__   c__ __t   r__s__

2. Underline the noun that names a thing.

   May I ride on the tractor?

3. Choose the verb that shows something happened in the past.

   Yesterday, Kat _____ some milk.

   had   has   is having

4. Write a word to take the place of the underlined word or words.

    he   she   it

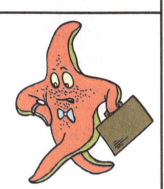

The car is full. → _____

5. Choose the correct word.

The socks (was / were) new.

The boy (was / were) late.

6. Put 2 questions together to make one.
   Example: When is the party? What should I bring?
   When is the party, and what should I bring?

When is your birthday? How old will you be?

_____

_____?

Lesson #20

1. Circle the words that tell *how many*.

   two fish   many children   several tables

   seven balls   few prizes   lots of animals

2. Put a comma between the words in the list.

   Fran wore her boots scarf hat and mittens.

3. Add a prefix. Write the missing word.

   pre-   re-   un-

   The _____ is when we do
   (game)
   warm-ups.

4. Write a sentence about the picture.
   Use the words in the box.

   | has   An   arms   octopus   eight |

   _____

   _____.

5. Write two more words that have the same root.

   bake   bakes   _____

   _____

6. Say each word. Write the number of syllables.

grandmother ___   glasses ___   ribbon ___

Lesson #21

1. Use the words in the box to make 3-syllable words.

   | bread | candle | time |
   | stick | winter | ginger |

   _____   _____

   _____

2. Write the correct end punctuation.

   Have you been to the new library___

   I have my own library card___

   Do you have one___

3. There are 2 words that should begin with a capital letter. Circle the letters that should be capital.

   On wednesday, casey has piano lessons.

4. **The letters *ay* make the long a sound.** Write the missing letters to spell words with the **long a** sound.
   Example: h __ __   h <u>a</u> y

   tr__ __   spr__ __   pl__ __

5. Draw a line under the proper noun.

   Let's go fishing with Grandpa!

6. Choose the verb that shows something will happen later.

   Tomorrow, they _____ on a hike.

   went   had   will go

Lesson #22

1. Use **he**, **she**, **it**, or **they** to take the place of the words below.

   the turtles _____

   Mr. Dennis → _____

2. Choose the correct word.

   We (is / are) going to the pool.

   Kyle (was / were) lost.

   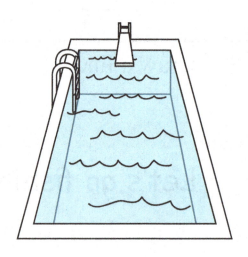

3. Circle the **adjectives** that tell *how many*.

   ten toes   three puppies   some toys

4. Put 2 questions together to make one.

   Do you want to go to the beach?
   Do you want to go shopping?

   _____

   _____

   _____?

5. Use the words in the box to make 3-syllable words.

   | fire | water | thunder |
   | fall | storm | fighter |

   _____   _____

   _____

6. Put a comma between the words in the list.

   Mario plays soccer baseball football and tennis.

Lesson #23

1. Which word means "**test again**"?

   testing   retest   pretest

2. Write a sentence to go with the picture. Use the words in the box.

eat   bugs   like   Bats   to

   _____

   _____.

3. **Add –ing to a verb to tell what is happening now.** Fill in the missing words.

   stir   pour   bake

   Alex and Max are _____ a cake.

   Alex is _____ in the flour and sugar.

   Max is _____ everything together with a big spoon.

4. Circle pictures of words that begin with **ch**.

5. Write the correct end punctuation.

I love ice cream__

We get it every Sunday__

Do you know that some people don't like it__

6. Write the months correctly.

january　_____

june　　_____

april　　_____

Lesson #24

1. Put an X over two words that are not spelled correctly.

    sae   play   May   wai   day

2. **A *noun* can show that something belongs to something.** Use an *apostrophe* and **s** ('s) to show this.

    Example: the school's playground

    Use an *apostrophe* and **s** to show the book belongs to the library.

    the _____ book
    (library)

3. Finish the story. Write a verb in each sentence. Use the words in the box.

    | is hiking   will come   went |

    Yesterday, Ben _____ on a trip.

    Today, Ben _____.

    Tomorrow, Ben _____ home.

4. Circle the best pronoun to complete the sentence.

   Mom read _____ a story.

   its   he   us

5. Choose the correct word.

   We (was / were) playing.

   The kittens (was / were) cute.

6. Circle the **adjectives** that tell what color.

   blue bike   brown puppy   purple coat

   orange pumpkin   green sock   black cat

   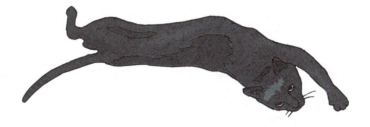

Lesson #25

1. Put a comma between the day and year.

   November 2 2011   April 9 2018

   January 4 2016   July 18 2014

2. Which word means "**without color**"?

   colorful   coloring   colorless

3. Write a sentence about the picture.
   Use the words in the box.

   | baby   crying   The |
   | stopped   little |

   _____

   _____ .

4. Add a suffix. Write the new word.

Base Word	-ed	-ing
turn	_____	_____
roar	_____	_____
lick	_____	_____

5. Say each word. Write the number of syllables.

grasshopper ___   swimming ___   boat ___

6. Write a sentence about the picture. Use the words in the box.

> bike every her
> rides day Megan

_____

_____.

Lesson #26

1. Check the sentences with the correct punctuation.

   ___ Wow, the cupcakes are hot!

   ___ We drank punch at the dance!

   ___ I'm late!

2. Study the list of words. Circle the words that should begin with a capital letter.

   friday   june   desk   september

   sally   bird   tuesday   i

3. **The letters *oa* make the long o sound**. Write the missing letters to spell words with the **long o** sound.

   t__ __d   b__ __t   g__ __l

4. Use an *apostrophe* and **s** to show the pencil belongs to Juan.

   _____ pencil
   (Juan)

5. Choose the verb that shows something is happening now.

   Sally _____ coffee.

   will make   is making   made

6. Write the best pronoun to complete the sentence.

   _____ coats are next to my coat.

   Our   Your

Lesson #27

1. Choose the correct word.

   We (was / were) playing in the snow.

   I (was / were) cold.

2. Put a comma between the names in the list.

   Amy Michelle Dana and Emily came to my birthday party.

3. Which word means **"full of color"**?

   colorful   re-color   colored

4. Write a sentence about the picture. Use the words in the box.

| picked   biggest   I   the   pumpkin |

_____

_____.

5. Circle the **adjectives** that tell about size.

big surprise   short chair   wide road

tiny mouse   huge lion   long rope

6. Use the words in the box to make 2-syllable words.

| kick   pig   ball |
| cow   pen   boy |

_____   _____

_____

Lesson #28

1. Add a suffix. Write the new word.

Base Word	-ed	-ing
fish	_____	_____
snow	_____	_____
cook	_____	_____

2. Circle the pictures that end with the **sh** sound.

3. Put the correct end punctuation in these sentences.

   Do you need to wear glasses___

   Computers can be fun to use___

   Mom loves to read to my little sister___

4. Circle the name that should begin with a capital letter. Write it correctly on the line.

Swimming is natalie's favorite sport.

_____

5. Choose a word to complete the sentence.

was   the   you   said

_____ cat drank all its milk.

My mom _____, "It's time to go home."

6. Underline the noun in this sentence.

Choose a sharp pencil.

Lesson #29

1. Draw a line to match each verb with the rest of its sentence.

   Yesterday, Dave   reads a book.

   Now, Dave   will take a nap.

   Later, Dave   played baseball.

2. Underline the pronouns in each sentence.

   I play the piano with her.

   The girls went to the store with them.

3. Choose the correct word.

   The days (was / were) hot.

   My shirt (was / were) torn.

4. **Adjectives can tell *how something feels.*** Circle the words that tell how something feels.

(warm) sun   cold ice   smooth skin

hard candy   soft blanket   bumpy road

5. Circle the sentence that is correct.

The puppy is sleeping

where are my keys?

Kerry got new skates.

6. Put a comma between the day and year.

November 18 2008   August 16 2017

September 9 2016   May 12 2014

Lesson #30

1. Which word means "**to play now**"?

   played   player   playing

   Which word means "**play in the past**"?

   played   player   playing

2. **Add –ing to a verb to tell what is happening now.**

   Fill in the missing words.

   show   write   ask

   The new student is _____ on the board.

   Miles is _____ the new student an empty desk.

3. Underline the group of words that makes a sentence.

   We have new costumes.

   A witch

   And a ghost.

4. Write the correct end punctuation.

Dad filled up the pool in the backyard___

Have you learned how to skateboard___

I can't wait to go to the baseball game___

5. Say each word. Write the number of syllables.

number ___   lizard ___   brush ___

6. Write the days correctly.

thursday_____

monday _____

Summer Solutions©   Common Core English Grammar & Mechanics 1

Common Core ENGLISH GRAMMAR & Mechanics 1

Answers to Lessons

	Lesson #1		Lesson #2		Lesson #3
1	Tuesday Saturday Monday	1	he they	1	brushed brushing watered watering barked barking
2	. ? ?	2	are are	2	(whale picture) (girls picture)
3	cup, hat, mouse	3	We have a <u>tall</u> family.	3	December Henry Chris Friday August
4	h<u>a</u>m f<u>a</u>n h<u>a</u>nd b<u>a</u>nd	4	June 10, 2007 March 30, 2016	4	✓ I am afraid of storms!
5	Mitch is mailing a letter to his grandmother.	5	A flat tire — does not roll. Tammy and Jessie — are sisters. Did you — remember your lunch?	5	mom, teacher, man
6	went	6	useless	6	family 3 mother 2 house 1

	Lesson #4		Lesson #5		Lesson #6
1	t<u>a</u>p<u>e</u> r<u>a</u>k<u>e</u> sn<u>a</u>k<u>e</u> c<u>a</u>n<u>e</u>	1	Julie, Tess, Pam, and Marta are my sisters.	1	Jamie read a book about tigers, bears, lions, and elephants.
2	will eat	2	playful	2	! ? .
3	he it	3	robbed robbing trimmed trimming dripped dripping	3	raked are falling will rake
4	I smell something good cooking in the oven.	4	My dad is my soccer coach.	4	(ricardo) was at the playground. Ricardo
5	are are	5	cl<u>oth</u> in<u>ch</u>	5	j<u>e</u>t t<u>e</u>nt b<u>e</u>d l<u>e</u>mon
6	(three) birds (many) children (one) candy cane (seven) dogs (few) kittens (five) rings	6	basketball 3 net 1 shoes 1	6	<u>Ohio</u> <u>Julie</u> <u>Maple Street</u>

	Lesson #7		Lesson #8		Lesson #9
1	she it they	1	hopped	1	b<u>ee</u> tr<u>ee</u> sh<u>ee</u>p <u>j</u>e<u>e</u>p
2	are is	2	raced wanted spelled	2	The <u>train</u> moves slowly.
3	(red) balloon (yellow) ball (pink) pen (green) fence (purple) grape (blue) sky	3	beginning 3 sunrise 2 rooster 2	3	Our team is winning, (and/so) the fans are cheering.
4	It is snowing, (and/so) I catch snowflakes on my tongue.	4	! ?	4	wears
5	June 3, 2005 May 21, 2013 September 10, 2017 July 5, 2011	5	(d)r. (t)orres gave the glasses to (n)ora.	5	he it
6	brush trash bush (trash and bush crossed out)	6	<u>The children</u> caught fireflies.	6	whisker whisper wheel (whisker and wheel crossed out)

	Lesson #10		Lesson #11		Lesson #12
1	is are	1	popcorn cupcake grapefruit	1	she they
2	(tiny) ants (huge) truck (tall) tree (big) house (small) dog (short) pencil	2	period question mark exclamation point	2	We went to the fair and rode the rides.
3	Karen had pink, yellow, blue, and orange hair clips.	3	(connor) (august) (monday)	3	is are
4	thankful	4	p<u>i</u>g b<u>i</u>b p<u>i</u>n d<u>i</u>g	4	A cat has <u>sharp</u> claws.
5	The red balloon flew away.	5	Uncle Pete *Charlotte's Web* Africa	5	June 6, 2017 February 14, 2015 May 4, 2012 August 1, 2014
6	spotted spotting shopped shopping	6	will have	6	bunch chips chick

Lesson #13		Lesson #14		Lesson #15	
1	useless	1	Friday Tuesday	1	Billy gave me a <u>blue</u> pencil.
2	<u>We play in the sand</u>.	2	My <u>brother</u> threw the ball.	2	Greg, Jack, Tim, and Doug are in my class.
3	showed clapped placed	3	will read is reading got	3	
4	seahorse starfish downtown	4	she it	4	preschool
5	. . ! (or .)	5	were was	5	A wind blew the sailboat.
6	k<u>ite</u> br<u>ide</u> v<u>ine</u> p<u>ipe</u>	6	We built a snowman and gave it a carrot nose.	6	napped napping begged begging stopped stopping

	Lesson #16		Lesson #17		Lesson #18
1	weekend bathtub football	1	they she	1	repaint
2	✓ . or ! ✓ ! ✓ ?	2	was were	2	<u>We ate ice cream</u>.
3	The teacher helped (betsy). Betsy	3	We went to the zoo and saw giraffes and elephants.	3	ripped ripping rolled rolling dragged dragging
4	f<u>o</u>x r<u>o</u>ck b<u>o</u>x m<u>o</u>p	4	(flat) pancakes (oval) track (round) peaches (wavy) line (long) snake (curved) road	4	! . ?
5	Our class went to the <u>park</u>.	5	Kathy has soccer practice on Tuesday, Wednesday, Thursday, and Saturday.	5	January June April
6	will eat	6	bro<u>th</u> pea<u>ch</u> too<u>th</u>	6	period 3 capital 3 alphabet 3

	Lesson #19		Lesson #20		Lesson #21
1	s<u>oa</u>p h<u>o</u>s<u>e</u> c<u>oa</u>t r<u>o</u>s<u>e</u>	1	(two) fish (seven) balls (many) children (few) prizes (several) tables (lots) of animals	1	candlestick gingerbread wintertime
2	May I ride on the <u>tractor</u>?	2	Fran wore her boots, scarf, hat, and mittens.	2	? . ?
3	had	3	pregame	3	On (w)ednesday, (c)asey has piano lessons.
4	It	4	An octopus has eight arms.	4	tr<u>ay</u> spr<u>ay</u> pl<u>ay</u>
5	were was	5	Answers will vary. baking, baker, baked	5	Let's go fishing with <u>Grandpa</u>.
6	When is your birthday, and how old will you be?	6	grandmother 3 glasses 2 ribbon 2	6	will go

	Lesson #22		Lesson #23		Lesson #24
1	they he	1	retest	1	~~sae~~ ~~wai~~
2	are was	2	Bats like to eat bugs.	2	library's
3	(ten) toes (three) puppies (some) toys	3	baking pouring stirring	3	went is hiking will come
4	Do you want to go to the beach or go shopping?	4		4	us
5	firefighter waterfall thunderstorm	5	! or . . ?	5	were were
6	Mario plays soccer, baseball, football, and tennis.	6	January June April	6	(blue) bike (orange) pumpkin (brown) puppy (green) sock (purple) coat (black) cat

Lesson #25		Lesson #26		Lesson #27	
1	November 2, 2011 January 4, 2016 April 9, 2018 July 18, 2014	1	✓ Wow, the cupcakes are hot! ✓ I'm late!	1	were was
2	colorless	2	friday june september sally tuesday i	2	Amy, Michelle, Dana, and Emily came to my birthday party.
3	The little baby stopped crying.	3	t<u>oa</u>d b<u>oa</u>t g<u>oa</u>l	3	colorful
4	turned turning roared roaring licked licking	4	Juan's	4	I picked the biggest pumpkin.
5	grasshopper 3 swimming 2 boat 1	5	is making	5	(big) surprise (tiny) mouse (short) chair (huge) lion (wide) road (long) rope
6	Megan rides her bike every day.	6	Your	6	kickball pigpen cowboy

Lesson #28	Lesson #29	Lesson #30
1. fished fishing snowed snowing cooked cooking	1. Yesterday, Dave — played baseball. Now, Dave — reads a book. Later, Dave — will take a nap.	1. playing played
2. (pictures: broccoli, brush, trash can, fish)	2. I play the piano with her. The girls went to the store with them.	2. writing showing
3. ? . .	3. were was	3. We have new costumes.
4. Swimming is (natalie's) favorite sport. Natalie's	4. (warm) sun (hard) candy (cold) ice (soft) blanket (smooth) skin (bumpy) road	4. . or ! ? ! or .
5. The said	5. Kerry got new skates.	5. number 2 lizard 2 brush 1
6. Choose a sharp pencil.	6. November 18, 2008 September 9, 2016 August 16, 2017 May 12, 2014	6. Thursday Monday